These Dark Days
A Poetry Chapbook

Hope Zane

For all the
Dirt-eaters, tired sleepers,
wine-drunk weepers;

For the beautiful ghosts
& anyone with a pulse.

Brother, are you strong?

CONTENTS

INTRODUCTION

This book has been a long time coming. I've tried to make a book of poetry before. In fact, I've started and stopped so many times over the years. It's interesting to look back at your own work: poems cast in amber, memorializing the person that you used to be, the things you used to love. I've changed, and my poems have changed too.

Among other developments, you may have noticed I've gotten into social media lately. "They" say that's the way it's done, and you need to do it in order to succeed. And honestly, I like it. I've taken to it like a fish to water. If you knew me back then, you know who I used to be: tangle-headed girl who prided herself on being outside the social media riffraff. If I'm being honest, I thought myself above it.

But times change. So do we.

Still, as much as I've embraced the age of Instagram and Twitter, I'm dismayed at some of it. I'm frustrated by the disposability of it. I'm frustrated by the thought of creating art-as-consumable, something to be quickly thumbed through on a break at work or while lying in bed wishing for sleep. Here today, gone and forgotten tomorrow.

I want something more permanent. I want to build things that last. A legacy, a map that leads back to the places we've come from and the people we've been. Something tangible that you can put on your shelf and feel with your hands. Something that is there with you through the good days and the bad, the bright days and the dark.

So here is my collection of poems. Some of them are old, some are new. They're poems about sex, love, and loss. About losing and finding who you are. Poems of nostalgia for other days——even the bad ones.

I hope you like them, and I hope they find a place close to your heart.

Danica the Pornographer

She of the blue-black hair cascading down yellow skin.

O cursed river, back of sinew
scent of spice and herbs.

O sacred woman.
twist of red lip, twinkle of intelligent eye

Woman, they want to paint you dark,
paint you victim.

Woman, they want to bury you in dirt & hide your bones

But they can't take the magic from you.
You have always been hero. You have always been gold.

Dirt Eater

How do you eat a mountain?
Mouthful by tired mouthful, face in the dirt.

How do you eat a mountain?
With your hair in your face & your hands over your eyes.

How do you eat a mountain?
With tea and crackers.

How do you eat a mountain?
You eat it naked, under the white light of a brilliant moon. You scoop it into your mouth with a silver spoon while your house burns down and your family cries.

How do you eat a mountain?
Never taking your eyes off your lover. You eat the dirt in your sleep, powdery and thick. It coats your throat and makes you cough in the night.

How do you eat a mountain?
With your wrists dripping water that came out of the Red Sea. You eat Adam's flesh, that dirt and blood combined.

How do you eat a mountain?
While everyone laughs, pointing and sneering at your mud-stained mouth.

You eat it like it's the last food on earth.
like your life depends on it.
like you're going to be shot.

You eat it like the world might end if you don't. Like there are demons in the closet with guns to your head and knives to your throat.

Like you're the last living woman with a pulse on this side of the Pacific.

Prayer No. 1

In my grief, I turn away from the one who can truly help.
Afraid of the shadows, I draw the curtains and blind the sun.
I curse the dark while chasing after rumors of light,
disappointed that none of them can save me from myself.

Wolves Look Like Sheep Look Like Wolves

1.

When I was a child,
I tasted my own tears and called it Nirvana.
Thought myself enlightened when all I learned
was how to hide my disappointment.

I pulled the wool over my own eyes over and over again,
then grieved at the darkness
and named it Loss.

2.

I've loved men who growled like wolves in the night,
turning shuddering away from my embrace

I've loved men who were more bird than man,
refusing to be caged by commitment
or possession
or singularity of place.
Their flight looked so sweet from the ground.

It took me years to realize
it was the freedom I loved.

The men were just something I could wrap my arms around.

3.

(I'm the wolf that killed the sheep, burned down the barn after it got dark.)

Extended Earth Metaphor

Member of the species who shows all the symptoms of being kind
so maybe this is why they keep slipping me counterfeits,
pulling my skirt up under the table,
sticking fingers into soil with no intention of staying for harvest

I was never your only.
Sometimes I could trace the resemblance in their faces
Other fields, golden like wheat or else black like night
to kiss with that same muddy mouth

I am not part of an interchangeable multitude
and yet we're all parts of a whole, so

Even if I am
a burned down house or
a country where no one lives anymore,

I am that certain house on the block that makes you shiver when you walk
past.
I am the fertile country of my grandmother's bones.

Things Change

I did love you in that house
with the burned down couch
We made love for hours
but I can't talk about it now

To the Girls Who Hang Out in the Mean Corners of the Internet

Soul-filled woman,

Handing them the sledge to break you down
Won't make them love you any more
Won't lessen the pain of the blows

They will still try to ruin you
They'll laugh when they do it
They'll tell their friends like it's a joke

The Matching Game

We didn't get it.

There was nothing *to* get.
not trying to enact racial politics with our bodies,
we weren't *doing* anything.

we paired brown with white
white with yellow
girl with girl
girl with boy with girl

We were innocent and naked,
sexy in our unknowing.

Other Prayer

Her hair shines in lamplight, hangs down to the floor. She kisses the hands of the old.

She brews water late into the night, makes the kettle whistle in the silence, utters strange prayers through hands splayed wide like the wings of doves.

She weaves apologies into her hair and tries to remember that nighttime is not a death sentence; the sun falling below the horizon in no way resembles the executioner's blade.

Mouths are beautiful to remind us to speak beautifully, to talk kindly and bless each other with our mouths. She reminds herself that fingers are so long and fragile to allow us to gently cup fallen birds' nests. They're soft so we can caress the curve of another's body.

Hands are for helping and feet are for walking gently on this earth.

She feels like the cup of tea tipped over on the shelf, Earl Grey leaking out and pooling at her feet.

She feels like the rabbit the gunshot killed.

Toothless Terrors

I leave coffee cups and tear stains everywhere I go. Night folds its lace gloves around my neck, makes me winged, makes me stand up like a woman.

But I'm soft. I crumple like morning, soft-gummed, all toothless, creased and full of ache.

The word *shelter* drips from a dishwater tongue like napalm. My prayers come in tones of the word *shatter*. My body is a soft-shelled apology, voice taken in a strip search.

I left my wallet and my love on a counter somewhere. I'm the snake skin left after the soul slithered away.

The dogs eat my lies in the night. I am made of mistake, clay split into the shape of a misused epilogue, tongue turned black. A misguided notion.

An Allegory of Abuse

The hungry dog didn't die; she got fed.
She ate a steady diet of bread and good meat,
and sharpened her teeth on things soft and hard.

The Ally and the Villain

You don't understand. I was an ally.

I would have been your last advocate. If you were standing at the Pearly Gates and Peter wouldn't let you in, I would have vouched for you. You've called me so many names through the years, and still...

I was kind to you.

I held the olive branch while you held the match, more kind than I needed to be. Let it be said: that has always been my fault. You snatched that shit and burned it. Of course you did. That's what villains do.

Fuck you, who held me late into the night, drying my tears all those lifetimes ago.
Fuck you for dirtying my good name. A court of our peers would find you guilty and me blameless.

So yes, now I'm blaspheming you all over the internet with words, which have always been my solace when I felt small and alone and no one would believe me.
They believe me now.

More important: I believe me now.

These Dark Days

Once in a rare moon, I still cry late into the night. My thoughts are my own, but my emotions suit me badly. I have no room for them. No room for this *want* that claws at my insides, shredding them like a cat in heat, screaming to get back to you.

I grab the feral creature, rein her in. Shove her into the pit of my belly and lock my ribs tight around her. I am smothering her, trying to make the awful yowling stop.

I never was built for happiness, but I shoved myself in and made it fit the mold.

Nevermind the ocean of longing that I still bleed. My wrists still bleed seawater from the gashes that we made long ago, lover. I held the knife, and you held my hand.

(I am broken and dark)

These days, I ignore the wounds that we so loved to lick together.

These days, I bind my arms tight with comforters and lace dresses. I ignore the love weeping through despite it all. I bind it tighter, pretend I'm whole.

I pretend you weren't always going to be the one.

Is this what being healthy feels like?
I'm sorry that I wanted it.

ABOUT THE AUTHOR

Hope Zane is a writer and artist living in Honolulu, Hawaii. She celebrates love and loss, beauty and pain through her work. She grew up on fantasy novels and indie music and thrives on finding magic in the mundane. She is always up to something. Follow her online @lovetincture or hopezane.com to find out what she's doing next.

Look out for Hope's debut novel, *The Poison Path*, in January 2019.

Sign up for her mailing list at hopezane.com/join to stay up to date when she releases new work.

Made in the USA
San Bernardino, CA
23 February 2019